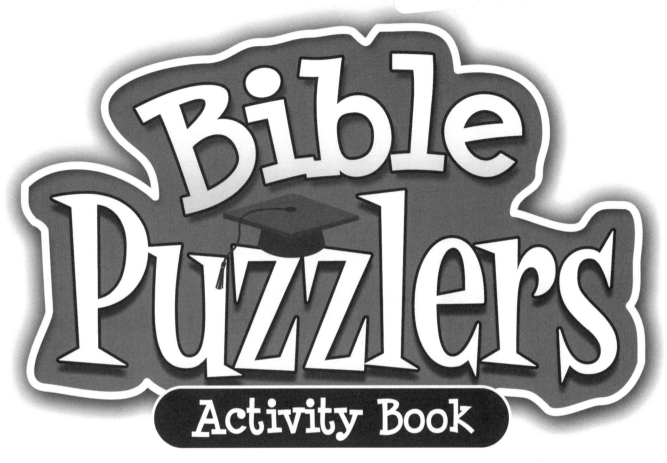

Written by Doris Mueller
Cover illustration by Christian Elden

Scripture taken from the **Holy Bible,** *New International Version®, NIV®*
Copyright © 1973, 1978, 1984, 2011 by Biblica, Inc.® Used by permission. All rights reserved worldwide.

305800214858

How It All Began

Scientists, historians, and archaeologists are always trying to learn more about how our earth began.

When you solve this puzzle,
you'll discover one thing we already know!
First, decode the words.
Then put them in the right order to read the Bible verse.

	1	2	3	4	5	6	7	8
A	T	O	G	R	N	E	C	N
B	D	I	N	V	E	S	H	D
C	B	E	A	E	N	H	A	E
D	G	N	E	T	E	H	G	I
E	A	T	S	S	N	E	L	E
F	I	R	E	R	T	O	T	H
G	I	A	H	E	D	N	N	G

___ ___ ___   ___ ___ ___ ___ ___ ___ ___ ___ ___
C3 A8 B8   C1 B5 D1 G1 B3 C5 F1 D2 D7

___ ___   ___ ___ ___   ___ ___ ___ ___ ___ ___ ___
B2 E5   E2 D6 F3   B7 E8 C7 B4 D3 G3 E3

___ ___ ___   ___ ___ ___ ___ ___   ___ ___ ___
A1 C6 G5   A6 E1 F2 F5 F8   G8 A2 G6

___ ___ ___   ___ ___ ___ ___ ___ ___ ___
D4 G4 C4   A7 F4 C2 G2 F7 C8 B1

___ ___ ___ ___ ___ ___ ___   1:1
A3 D5 A5 E6 B6 G1 E4

____ ____ _____ _____ _____

_____ _____ _____ _____ _____ .

_____ 1:1

(Answer on page 16)

A Scrambled Riddle

The scrambled words below are from the life of Moses.

Unscramble each group of letters
and write the words on the dashes.
Use the numbered letters to answer the question
at the bottom of the page.

S S O E M
(His mother hid him in a basket.)

___ ___ ___ ___ ___
4   13   2

R A N O A
(Moses' brother.)

___ ___ ___ ___ ___
        8

V E S A L
(A person who is owned by another person.)

___ ___ ___ ___ ___
  1   11

P Y T E G
(God's people were slaves in this land.)

___ ___ ___ ___ ___
  12 5 6 3

G A P L E U
(Ten of these bad things happened in Egypt
because Pharaoh would not obey God.)

___ ___ ___ ___ ___ ___
9 10

E P A C L A
(Where Moses lived with Pharaoh's daughter.)

___ ___ ___ ___ ___ ___
            7

What was the demand Moses made of Pharaoh?

___ ___ ___ ___ ___ ___ ___ ___ ___ ___ ___ ___ ___! Exodus 5:1
 1 2 3   4 5   6 7 8 9 10 11   12 13

(Answer on page 16)

Bible Brothers

Can you pick the correct brother from the list for the following Bible characters?

(Hint: Look up the Bible verse if you get stuck!)

Esau	Shem	Abel
Isaac	Aaron	Jonathan
Joseph	Solomon	

1. Cain killed his brother _____. (Genesis 4:8)

2. Ishmael was the half-brother of _____. (Genesis 25:9)

3. Jacob and _____ were twins. (Genesis 25:25-26)

4. Moses had a brother named _____. (Exodus 4:14)

5. Saul's daughter Michal had a brother named _____. (1 Samuel 14:49)

6. _____, Ham, and Japheth were the sons of Noah. (Genesis 9:18)

7. Absalom and _____ were King David's sons. (2 Samuel 12:24)

8. _____ and Benjamin were the sons of Jacob and Rachel. (Genesis 35:22-24)

Just for fun: Try to unscramble this tongue twister about Jacob's twin.

M E W U S E A A U S E A S

I   _ _ _   _ _ _ _ ,   _ _ _ _   _ _.

(Answer on page 16)

Kings of Judah
Word Search

See if you can find and circle the names
of these ten Old Testament kings.

Remember, the names may be written
up, down, left, right, or diagonally.

Rehoboam	Josiah	Asa
Abijah	Ahaz	Amon
Hezekiah	Zedekiah	Joash	Jotham

```
R   X   H   A   J   I   B   A
H   E   Z   E   K   I   A   H
H   O   H   D   L   A   S   M
A   H   J   O   T   H   A   M
I   O   U   K   B   J   N   N
K   Q   H   S   A   O   J   R
E   A   M   O   N   S   A   K
D   N   J   R   F   I   F   M
E   R   B   G   T   A   D   V
Z   A   H   A   S   H   G   M
```

(Answer on page 16)

Bible Birdwatching

Do you like to watch birds at your feeder
or when you walk in the park?
Did you ever look for birds in your Bible?

See if you know what each bird is
by its description and scrambled letters.
Then look up the Bible verses and see if you can find birds there!

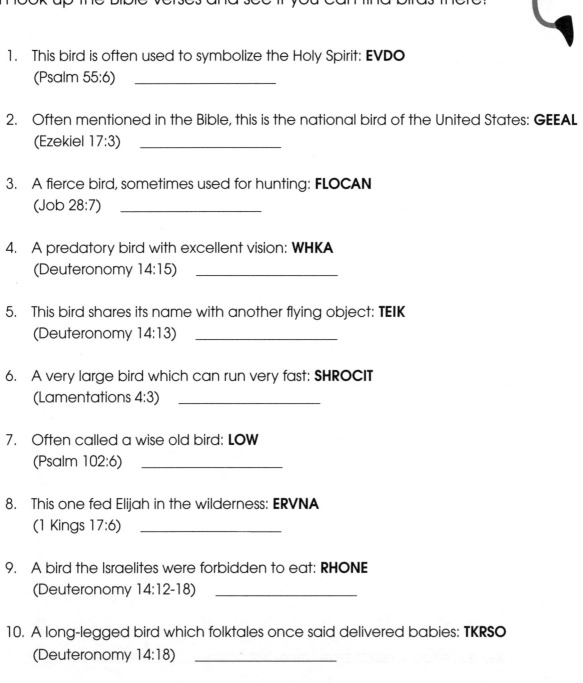

1. This bird is often used to symbolize the Holy Spirit: **EVDO**
   (Psalm 55:6) _____

2. Often mentioned in the Bible, this is the national bird of the United States: **GEEAL**
   (Ezekiel 17:3) _____

3. A fierce bird, sometimes used for hunting: **FLOCAN**
   (Job 28:7) _____

4. A predatory bird with excellent vision: **WHKA**
   (Deuteronomy 14:15) _____

5. This bird shares its name with another flying object: **TEIK**
   (Deuteronomy 14:13) _____

6. A very large bird which can run very fast: **SHROCIT**
   (Lamentations 4:3) _____

7. Often called a wise old bird: **LOW**
   (Psalm 102:6) _____

8. This one fed Elijah in the wilderness: **ERVNA**
   (1 Kings 17:6) _____

9. A bird the Israelites were forbidden to eat: **RHONE**
   (Deuteronomy 14:12-18) _____

10. A long-legged bird which folktales once said delivered babies: **TKRSO**
    (Deuteronomy 14:18) _____

(Answer on page 16)

Famous Pairs

A Double Whammy!

```
F  O  R  L  E  B  A  G  O  D  S  O  L  O
V  E  D  T  H  E  W  O  R  E  L  D  T  H
A  T  H  J  E  L  G  A  S  V  E  G  H  I
S  O  N  E  E  A  N  A  D  O  N  O  L  Y
S  O  N  H  T  Z  U  H  A  T  W  L  H  O
E  V  C  E  R  B  E  E  L  I  E  I  V  E
A  A  R  O  N  S  A  B  R  A  H  A  M  I
R  N  H  I  M  S  H  A  E  L  L  T  N  O
T  P  E  R  I  D  E  L  I  L  A  H  S  H
B  U  T  H  A  V  V  E  E  T  E  R  N  A
L  L  I  F  E  R  E  N  A  L  D  R  L  I
F  E  H  S  I  F  E  N  T  B  H  A  N  T
```

FIRST, write the second person of each pair on the dashes.
NEXT, find and circle the names you've written in the puzzle above.
They may be up, down, left, right, or diagonal.
LAST, use the leftover letters to write a Bible verse on the lines
at the bottom of the page. (Not all of the letters will be used.)
We often call it "the Bible in a nutshell."

(1 Samuel 17:4)   1. David/ — — — — — — — —

(Judges 16:4)   2. Samson/ — — — — — — —

(Genesis 3:20)   3. Adam/ — — —

(Genesis 4:1-2)   4. Cain/ — — — — —

(Exodus 4:14)   5. Moses/ — — — — — —

(Genesis 25:25-26)   6. Jacob/ — — — —

(Genesis 17:5)   7. Sarah/ — — — — — — —

(Jonah 1:17)   8. Jonah/ — — — —

(Genesis 29:9)   9. Jacob/ — — — — — — —

(1 Kings 16:31)   10. Ahab/ — — — — — — —

_____ _____ _____ _____ _____ _____

_____ _____ _____ _____ _____ , _____ _____

_____ _____ _____ _____ _____ _____

_____ _____ _____ _____ .   John 3:16

(Answer on page 16)

People Who Spoke for God

God speaks to us in many ways.
He once spoke in a burning bush;
at other times He spoke in a still, small voice.
Through the ages, God has called people
of faith to speak for Him.

Hidden in this puzzle are the names of people
in the Old Testament who spoke for God,
even if that made them unpopular or put them in danger.
Find and circle them.

Moses	Joel	Jonah	Micah	Elijah
Elisha	Amos	Samuel	Isaiah	Malachi
Nahum	Hosea	Joshua	Daniel	

```
A Y J O N A H O S
M E L I J A H A U
O M I C A H M M U
S H S T S U P E A
D A N I E L K E A
M I Y L J O E L U
M A L A C H I I H
W S E S O M O S S
R I N A H U M H O
D H O S E A S A J
```

Now use the leftover letters to write a command God gave one of His spokesmen.

_____ _____ _____ _____ _____ .   Ezekiel 2:7

(Answer on page 16)

A Rule to Live By

If you can work through this maze of letters, you'll find the rule.

Begin at the top arrow.
The letters will follow each other up, down, left, right, and diagonally to create words to a Bible verse.
End at the bottom arrow.

D	L	M	O	X	A	B	Y	S	M	N	O	P
F	O	T	L	O	N	E	R	Q	W	A	S	L
A	Y	M	P	T	L	E	T	T	O	H	P	W
B	O	D	J	K	H	L	M	R	A	B	A	E
D	B	C	W	W	U	O	Y	T	R	S	D	Y
N	X	I	U	O	A	P	R	A	G	B	T	O
U	I	L	D	H	P	X	C	T	J	R	O	Y
M	L	O	P	E	A	V	E	H	E	D	L	O
V	K	B	I	N	W	A	T	R	E	M	N	U
P	G	S	F	O	U	L	W	N	B	C	V	Y

D___ ____ _____ _____

_____ _____ _____

_____ _____ _____ _____ U .   Matthew 7:12

(Answer on page 16)

Page 9

Wacky Words

Can you decode these words or phrases
by the way the letters or symbols are arranged?

Example: busines
(You knew that was "unfinished business," didn't you?)
Okay, let's go!

1. Do you recognize this hymn?   theshebringingaves

    _____.

2. Christians believe in: death/life

    _____

3. In Ephesians Jesus is called this:

    S

    T

    O N E

    _____.

4. When Jesus went out into the desert to pray, He was also:

    it all   getting

    _____.

5. You've probably heard that: wrongwrong≠right

    _____

6. Think Christmas!   Noe____

    _____

7. When dangers lurk, there may be: 12safety345

    _____.

8. Jesus wants His followers to do this:

    G   o   s   p   e   l

    _____

You Have His Word on It!

The Bible is filled with God's promises.
See if you can reveal this one.

The first letter is circled.
Move up, down, or diagonally to read
a 5-word, 20-letter Bible promise.

Use each letter only once.
Write the promise on the line after the clue.

```
Y   V   I   E

R   E   I   C

U   W   L   E

O   D   L   R

Y   S   N   X

D  (A)  K   A
```

Clue: God answers prayer.

_____ _____ _____ _____ _____ .   John 16:24

(Answer on page 16)

Bible Who-Dunnits

See how many of these "who-dunnits" you can solve on your own.
Then you can check the Bible references for any that are left.
The idea is to match the "who" with the "dunnit" by putting
the letter of the correct answer in the space.

Ready?

____1. Denied (disowned) Jesus even after he'd sworn never to do so. (Matthew 26:69-75)

a. Judas

____2. Persecuted the Christians until he was struck down and blinded. (Acts 9:1-4)

b. Peter

____3. Betrayed Jesus for money. (Luke 22:4-5)

c. Saul/Paul

____4. Refused to believe Jesus had risen from the dead until he had proof. (John 20:24-26)

d. Thomas

____5. Tried to cheat by pretending to give a larger gift to the church than he really did. (Acts 5:1-4)

e. Herod

____6. Gave Jesus up to be crucified even though he knew Jesus was innocent. (Matthew 27:24-26)

f. Ananias

____7. Had John the Baptist beheaded to please Salome. (Matthew 14:6-10)

g. Simon of Cyrene

____8. Carried Jesus' cross to Golgotha. (Matthew 27:32)

h. Pilate

(Answer on page 16)

Loyalty to God

First, add and subtract to find the new numbers for the code.

Then solve the puzzle to read what Jesus said is the greatest commandment.

Add 3 to each number below:

A	D	E	G	H	I	L	O
10	12	22	79	94	62	51	16

Subtract 2 from each number below:

R	S	T	U	V	W	Y
96	64	23	25	79	62	13

___ ___ ___ ___   ___ ___ ___ ___ ___
21 97 19 23   62 97 13 54 21

___ ___ ___ ___   ___ ___ ___
54 19 77 25   21 97 25

___ ___ ___ ___   ___ ___ ___
54 19 94 15   21 97 11

___ ___ ___   ___ ___ ___ ___
82 19 15   60 65 21 97

___ ___ ___   ___ ___ ___
13 54 54   21 97 11

___ ___ ___ ___ ___.   Mark 12:30 KJV
97 25 13 94 21

(Answer on page 16)

Bible Towns and Cities

When you have found all of these New Testament cities,
the first 58 leftover letters will make a Bible verse.

Write the letters in order;
then check yourself by looking up Psalm 127:1.

D	U	N	M	E	L	A	S	U	R	E	J
A	L	E	R	Y	T	E	S	S	T	E	H
M	E	L	O	H	R	D	W	A	R	T	C
A	H	E	E	G	A	N	T	I	O	C	H
S	S	N	A	O	E	V	C	E	R	T	H
C	S	Z	E	C	M	H	I	T	Y	T	H
U	A	H	E	C	O	R	I	N	T	H	T
S	W	A	T	C	R	H	M	E	N	S	E
T	N	O	L	Y	B	A	B	A	N	D	R
G	U	A	R	D	I	N	V	A	I	N	A
N	Q	U	N	S	U	S	R	A	T	X	Z
B	A	S	V	L	T	D	M	T	W	O	A
L	P	R	E	O	S	C	N	P	Z	O	N

JERUSALEM	GAZA	NAZARETH
JERICHO	DAMASCUS	TYRE
BABYLON	ANTIOCH	CORINTH
ROME	ATHENS	TARSUS

_____ _____ _____ _____ _____

_____ _____ _____ _____ _____ _____ _____ .

(Answer on page 16)

Where Is the Holy Spirit?

Find and circle the listed words.
Then read a hidden message using the letters you have not circled.
On the lines below, write the Bible verse that reminds us
how close the Holy Spirit really is.

E	N	C	O	U	R	A	G	E	S
D	O	Y	O	U	N	U	O	E	T
K	N	O	W	T	I	H	S	A	T
Y	O	U	R	D	H	S	B	O	D
Y	I	S	E	A	E	T	S	E	M
P	L	S	E	N	L	O	D	F	T
S	H	E	T	H	P	R	A	Y	S
E	O	I	L	Y	S	S	E	P	I
R	W	R	I	T	W	H	L	O	I
I	S	I	N	Y	O	U	W	H	O
P	M	Y	O	U	H	A	V	E	R
S	T	R	O	F	M	O	C	E	C
N	E	I	V	E	D	F	R	O	M
I	G	O	D	X	K	A	M	W	F

WITNESSES	ENCOURAGES	LEADS
INSPIRES	HELPS	COMFORTS
PRAYS	GUIDES	

_____ _____ _____ _____ _____ _____ _____

_____ _____ _____ _____ _____, _____ _____ _____ _____,

_____ _____ _____ _____ _____ _____ _____? 1 Corinthians 6:19

(Answer on page 16)   Page 15

Answer Page

Page 2—In the beginning God created the heavens and the earth. *Genesis 1:1*

Page 3—Moses, Aaron, Slave, Egypt, Plague, Palace   Let my people go! *Exodus 5:1*

Page 4—1. Abel 2. Isaac 3. Esau 4. Aaron 5. Jonathan 6. Shem 7. Solomon 8. Joseph
Tongue Twister: I saw Esau, Esau me.

Page 5

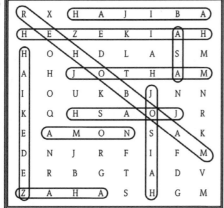

Page 6—1. dove 2. eagle 3. falcon 4. hawk 5. kite
6. ostrich 7. owl 8. raven 9. heron 10. stork

Page 7

1. Goliath
2. Delilah
3. Eve
4. Abel
5. Aaron
6. Esau
7. Abraham
8. Fish
9. Rachel
10. Jezebel

For God so loved the world that he gave his one and only Son, that whoever believes in him shall not perish but have eternal life. *John 3:16*

Page 8

You must speak my words. *Ezekiel 2:7*

Page 9—Do to others what you would have them do to you. *Matthew 7:12*

Page 10—1. Bringing in the Sheaves 2. life after death 3. cornerstone 4. getting away from it all 5. two wrongs don't make a right 6. Noel 7. safety in numbers 8. spread the Gospel

Page 11—Ask and you will receive. *John 16:24*

Page 12—1. b
2. c
3. a
4. d
5. f
6. h
7. e
8. g

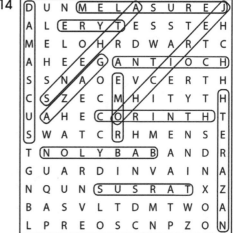

Page 13—Thou shalt love the Lord thy God with all thy heart. *Mark 12:30 KJV*

Page 14

Unless the Lord watches over the city the watchmen stand guard in vain.

Page 15—Do you not know that your body is a temple of the Holy Spirit, who is in you, whom you have received from God?